ESSENTIALISM:

Your Guide to The Power of Less

Set your Mind with Practical Tips to Make Your Life More Manageable and Become a Happy Essentialist

MARK CREED

Text Copyright © Mark Creed

All rights reserved. No part of this guide may be reproduced in any form without permission in writing from the publisher except in the case of brief quotations embodied in critical articles or reviews.

Legal & Disclaimer

The information contained in this book and its contents is not designed to replace or take the place of any form of medical or professional advice; and is not meant to replace the need for independent medical, financial, legal or other professional advice or services, as may be required. The content and information in this book has been provided for educational and entertainment purposes only.

The content and information contained in this book has been compiled from sources deemed reliable, and it is accurate to the best of the Author's knowledge, information and belief. However, the Author cannot guarantee its accuracy and validity and cannot be held liable for any errors and/or omissions. Further, changes are periodically made to this book as and when needed. Where appropriate and/or necessary, you must consult a professional (including but not limited to your doctor, attorney, financial advisor or such other professional advisor) before using any of the suggested remedies, techniques, or information in this book.

Upon using the contents and information contained in this book, you agree to hold harmless the Author from and against any damages, costs, and expenses, including any legal fees potentially resulting from the application of any of the information provided by this book. This disclaimer applies to any loss, damages or injury caused by the use and application, whether directly or indirectly, of any advice or information presented, whether for breach of contract, tort, negligence, personal injury, criminal intent, or under any other cause of action.

You agree to accept all risks of using the information presented inside this book.

You agree that by continuing to read this book, where appropriate and/or necessary, you shall consult a professional (including but not limited to your doctor, attorney, or financial advisor or such other advisor as needed) before using any of the suggested remedies, techniques, or information in this book.

Table of Contents

Chapter 1: Why Our World Is Unnecessarily Complicated . 1

Chapter 2: What Is Essentialism? 7

Chapter 3: What It Takes To Become An Essentialist 12

Chapter 4: How To Maintain Your Mind 21

Chapter 5: Why Less Is More In All Aspects Of Life 27

Chapter 6: Making Time For Free Time 37

Chapter 7: Say Goodbye To All The Time Vampires 44

    Here Are A Few Suggestions And Tips: 48

Chapter 8: Giving 100% 51

Chapter 9: Reframe All Negative Thoughts 57

Chapter 10: Living In The Present Moment 62

Chapter 11: Looking Into The Mirror 66

Chapter 12: The Magic Of Positive Attitude 71

Chapter 13: The Psychology Of Clutter 75

    Why We Keep Things 75
        Monetary Value 76
        Sentimental Collections 76
        A Possible Future Need 77

Chapter 14: Accessing Your Subconscious 80

Chapter 15: Have A Clearer Head 85

    Time And Space To Focus On Health, Hobbies, And Learning... 86
    Less Focus On Material Possessions And Competition 88

A Greater Sense Of Happiness, Confidence, And Contentment 89

Chapter 16: What About Today? 92

Chapter 17: Mindfulness Meditation 96

Chapter 18: Take Back Your Thoughts............................. 102

Chapter 19: Importance Of Essentialism To Your Health 108

Chapter 20: Tackle Your Problems Head-On 113

Start By Facing Reality 114
Facing Your Problems, Overcoming Your Challenges 115

Conclusion 118

CHAPTER 1:

Why Our World is Unnecessarily Complicated

No, it is not just you. The world is much more complex than it used to be. Think back to the 80's, just four decades ago. The computer did not yet exist, the internet was a decade away from being discovered, and films were the only way cameras captured memories. There are so many sociological and technological changes that have happened to Mother Earth since the 1980s.

The thing is, advancements in technology have naturally made once not-so-complicated systems become unnecessarily complex, which has made it almost impossible to predict what will occur next.

With all this conscious awareness of the unknown, society has placed exuberate amounts of worth into physical objects. Our lives are literally packed with stuff – iPads, furniture, jewelry, toys, cars, clothing, books, bags, etc. The list goes on and on. The reality of it is, these possessions eventually become a part of us, creating an extension of ourselves. We utilize the things we own to signal to others and ourselves of who we are, who we wish to be, and where we belong. Long after we leave this planet, our stuff becomes our legacy, which gives the idea to so many that what we own is the essence of our lives.

What kind of way is this to live? When you read it like this, I am sure you are flabbergasted as to how you too have fallen into the pit of physical objects controlling our lives and establishing our self-worth. Thanks to the large amounts of things we all own; it creates a rift in humankind that society may never seem to shake.

Childhood and Adolescence

The relationship we have with items starts very early on. By the age of two, we know that we possess things as our own. And by the age of six, we place value on certain items. One can genuinely say that part of our attachment issues relates directly to our natural psyche.

As time goes on, ownership will turn into envious feelings in some people. When we play with our friends as kids, we discover other toys that we desire and want. Children naturally have a very intense relationship with attachment to items. We strongly believe that our belongings have an essence that is unique during this age, which inconsequently reappears during our teens and adulthood stages as memorabilia, artworks, and heirlooms.

As children grow into teens, possessions begin to play a role as a crutch to lean on. While those that received flattering feedback from peers value material items less, those with a low self-esteem value items much more. They provided those with a lack of confidence a sense of worthiness and accomplishment.

Adulthood

As teenagers mature into young adults, items such as the purchase of their first car, along with similar things, become a symbol of their developing identities. Many people view vehicles, for instance, as a prominent extension of themselves.

As adults continue to grow and mature, material objects also rise in determining their identity as they become part of our memories and core relationships. The thing is, how we view the things in our lives depends on the amount of esteem and confidence we have. This absorption of objects within identity is more than just a classic metaphor. Certain parts of the brain have been identified as being directly linked to how we perceive ourselves through our involvement and ownership of physical things. Our possessions are also a way to signal others to distinguish things about ourselves.

Loss of Belongings

Since we as a society have been taught and are scientifically drawn to the possession of things as providing ourselves with value, when we accumulate more items, our identities become strongly infused with these things. When folks lose their possessions in tragedies and disasters, I am sure you can imagine how much grief goes into the loss of those items.

Yet, there are tons of times that people do willfully dispose of certain things – from leaving home, to moving, to creating a new life after divorce, etc. Ridding yourself of particular objects is seen as starting with a clean slate.

Why I Created This Book

You are probably curious as to why I created a book about essentialism since I am stating an argument that having possessions is okay with society and is driven in us naturally as well. The biggest issue with our world today, however, is that we have an obsession with possessions. Instead of having essential things in our lives, we find ourselves lost in the extraordinarily useless stuff that actually tarnishes our worth instead of building value to it.

Within the remaining chapters of this book, you will find areas I am sure you will relate to as we discuss how obsession with possession can take a hold of your life in an overall negative way and how learning and adopting even just a tiny amount of essentialism can help you to turn your life around in positively drastic ways.

The last chapter of this book brings to light how adopting essentialism in my life finally helped me to get back on track to where I wanted my life to go, and how it changed not only my life but the people who are important to me as well.

Essentialism is not as much of a lifestyle choice as it is a positive choice you can learn to understand and choose for yourself to be able to thrive and finally find ultimate contentment and happiness among the chaos of the possessions, we are quite literally drowning in. I wish you luck on your journey to learning about essentialism, how to change your mindset and develop a life you can only dream of now, but soon make into reality!

CHAPTER 2:

What is Essentialism?

It is certainly no secret that the world we live in is a chaotic one and continues to rise to the level of madness. We are taught that working more is crucial, that saying 'yes' to everything we are asked is expected, so we attempt to do it **all**. I like to refer to the world as a center of madness, because I, among – I am sure – thousands of others, feel they are living in a truly mad world.

The way many of us live our lives today has become detrimental to our health, well-being, sanity and happiness. We live in a monopoly that requires us to do more, get more, fit more, and strive for more, more, MORE.

The thing is, before any of us can rework our behaviors, we have to learn the basics of how we ended up here in the first place. Our society is literally consumed in the desire for more, which is why we constantly take on additional things. We are faced with an outrageous relationship between consumerism, social media, and smart devices. While these things are not essentially bad for us, when they come together in negative ways, it leads to unintended results. We have become engulfed with the pursuit of more and the only way to overcome this is to adopt a completely new mindset to do the things that are only essential to our lives.

Essentialism, in other words, is not a tip, technique, or tactic, but a mindset.
As we continuously find ourselves being stretched thin, feeling underutilized and overworked, tired of the momentum, and feeling like our lives were hijacked for the agenda of another, then the road to essentialism is what our society needs to begin the process of slowing down such a chaotic world and to get back to the basics.

Essentialism engages us in doing less, but doing better in what we are doing, so we are still making valuable contributions. No, this is not a method of getting more done in the least amount of time and it does not promote being lazy and getting less accomplished.

The "essential" core of the idea of essentialism is getting back to the absolute basics, striving to meet our needs and not over-saturate our lives with things that we think we need or desire.

History of Essentialism

Essentialism in the educational world started as an unfavorable answer to that of progressivism, which is the value of experimental learning. In 1938, the Essentialist's Committee for the Advancement of Education got together in an attempt to get the entire educational system to take on a "back to the basics" approach. Philosophy, however, failed to gain momentum till Sputnik made its way into society in the late 1950s. Essentialism then became a driving force in the education system and continued to be popular until the 1980s.

The 1980s introduced an entire method of thought called non-essentialism, which came from the idea to assist America with the issues it was facing at the current time.

Essentialism in Education

Essentialism in the world of education requires teachers and professors to embed values traditional to the respect of the classroom. The entire class focuses on traditional disciplines, such as literature, history, science, math, etc. Children are required from schools to master these basic techniques and gradually continue forward as they learned detailed, more complex knowledge.

Thanks to essentialism, classrooms are not only teacher-oriented but the entire base of instruction is based on what the students need to learn rather than just what intrigues them. Lessons are taught to groups of students in a passive manner where they are required to listen to the teacher and take notes without the interruption of too many questions.

Some of the benefits of essentialism in the classroom are:

- Better sense of self-discipline
- Avid proficiency in basic skills
- Discipline in work ethic
- Building of stronger knowledge foundations

I am by no means suggesting our educational system is perfect but it does help in developing the basic aspects of a healthy character.

Chapter 3:

What It Takes to Become an Essentialist

As you have read, essentialism is **essentially** an upgrade on the concept of minimalism, which is living more with less. While there are many folks who have adopted the minimalistic way of life by quitting jobs they hated, donating clothes they no longer wear, stripping down their diets to raw fruits and veggies, they have actually missed the entire point of minimalism. They have failed to optimize what it means to willfully do less in the quest for better results.

The Artistry of Essentialism

You will find that you will only be able to contribute yourself to the highest of things when you give yourself permissions to quit attempting to do everything and say yes to everyone. The beauty of the essentialist concept is that it stands in opposition of what we tend to naturally do in our society today, which is to do it all, strive for more, and attempt to squeeze every ounce of life from each and every day. But to what end?

Why:

Do we overlook schedules, knowing it could take weeks to do what we wish to accomplish in a few hours?

Do we feel the desire to impress people with a billion extra-curricular activities?

Why are we fighting so darn hard to do so much?

The reality of it all is that we naturally have the tendency to bite off much more than we can chew and become impatiently frustrated when we choke. The good news? There is a way out that involves viewing the bigger picture of life in a much simpler fashion, which trickles down to our daily list of commitments.

What It Takes to Be an Essentialist

First, you need to realize that essentialism is not a restricted action or one decision to live with less. The core of being an essentialist is to embrace the lifestyle to seek out what genuinely matters and to let everything else contributing to the distracting fog of our lives go.

There are three main strategies to successfully becoming an essentialist:

Identify Non-essentialists

Non-essentialists are the total opposite of essentialists, of course. There are many signs that you can look for in yourself as well as others to become an expert at spotting behaviors that lead to a tangible lack of progress in the pursuit of more meaningful outcomes:

Feelings of exhaustion and being overwhelmed

Unsure whether the right things were achieved

Puts too much in their plate and work suffers due to this

Reacts to the most pressing things

Focuses more on the pursuit of more

Ask themselves all the time how they fit into the world

Thinks they have to do things

Is "all the things" to all the people

Master the Art of "No"

There are essentially two sides to being an avid essentialist. One side is exclusively saying yes only to things that matter to you and persistently saying no to anything that could potentially cloud your way of life. Genuine essentialists say yes on very rare occasions but are always ready to use no.

Stop viewing "no" as negative. In fact, utilizing that word more in all aspects of everyday life can assist you in keeping sane and filtering out the nonsense that fogs up your life. Saying "no," as we are all aware, can be rather challenging at times.

Most of us, myself included, would rather say "yes" when we are in a pinch and attempt to backtrack at a later time. Instead of holding true to ourselves and saying "no," we take the easy way out and allow our time to be gobbled up by people and other things that really do not deserve it. Learning the artform of saying "no" is one of the best ways to gain traction in your life to help you achieve your biggest goals.

Fall in Love with the Idea that Less is Better

I am sure from time to time you ponder over the idea of needing to do less while achieving better, more impactful results. Where people get lost, however, is what they are willing to give up to accomplish this feat.

It's easy to read something positively impactful, highlight the mind-blowing thoughts and feel as though you have made progress in your pursuit of a better life. But, when you start to ponder over how to implement those ideas into your everyday life, it can be daunting.

For me, when I was trying to figure out how to go about doing multiple things, I always asked myself "How can I do ____ AND ____ instead of ____." This is when I had a light bulb moment and realized I was living like a non-essentialist. I realized I was asking myself totally wrong questions that only led me down a path to burning myself out.

The key to letting go of old ways and habits is being willing to fall in love with the idea that less is, indeed, better. Instead, ask yourself questions like these:

What can I willingly devote my life to?

What projects are key to making the biggest difference?

In what way can I dedicate myself to a smaller number of projects and still receive better results?

Principles of Essentialism

Many of us are always tempted to pile our plates with more than we can truly handle, mainly because of how challenging it is to let opportunities fall to the side. Each request, invitation, and proposal feel somewhat special and we make it seem that we must promise ourselves to do it in an attempt to bring more importance, reward, and pleasure into our lives. But we are only clouding what we should genuinely be focused on.

When we lose sight of goals and our well-being, we enter into this realm, thinking we will always find ways to squeeze new things demanded of us into our already hectic schedule. We neglect that we say yes to too many projects that are not essential to our lives and we find ourselves in a mess of stress that takes a detrimental toll on our health, relationships, and overall performance.

Here are more key points that apply to becoming an essentialist and help to improve productivity and well-being:

Power of Choice

We usually let others have the power to determine how our time is spent when we forget we have the power to make a choice. Essentials find empowerment by deciding themselves what they need to do and don't do with their precious time.

Value of Criteria

Essentialists look at all requirements of things before agreeing to them, not just the minimum requirements. These are known as "extreme criteria" and involves one to evaluate all possibilities, such as if that is how they wish to spend their time, if the opportunity is ideal for them, or if that opportunity can leverage their goals and talents, etc. Like we have said before, if you cannot find a clear "yes," it should be a blatant and clear "no."

Reality of Trade-Offs

When we choose to do one thing, this requires us to let go of another, even if the other things are, indeed, essential. The more we commit ourselves to doing, the less room we have in our lives for the more important things, such as exercise, relationships, family, and passions. Those who live the essentialist way of life weigh the opportunities presented to them and view the trade-offs they make, this ensures they choose the right things more often which enables them to have more time in general.

Momentum of Focus

For ten things that non-essentialists do, essentialists perform one. As a society, we are only diffusing the energy we have by distracting ourselves with a plethora of unimportant things instead of focusing our energies on a few crucial things. This allows them to gain the momentum they need to be successful and perform well. If you constantly feel spread too thin, this is a red flag that it is time to let go of some commitments and relieve yourself to harness that precious focus.

Clarity is Crucial

Essentialists say no around 90 percent of the time when certain requests come their way. They live to make it clear as to what they should be doing and know the reason why they say no. When you have a clarity of what you are doing and the **why** that lies underneath it, it makes it a heck of a lot easier to filter out the hundreds of other things that could take a toll on your life and waste your time.

If essentialists want this type of clarity, they must ask themselves every day the difficult questions that many of us others avoid, as well as make trade-offs and exercise their self-discipline muscle. Essentialists are extremely aware that it is indeed worth directing most of their attention to the vital 10 percent of opportunities that make sense for **them** and **their** lives.

Chapter 4:

How to Maintain Your Mind

Once you have freed your mind from the noise that tends to build up there, it is important to maintain it. Think of your brain as you would your muscles. You don't just build them and keep them; you need to continuously work to maintain them.

There are lots of little ways to maintain a clutter-free mind. The first thing is to avoid accumulating more clutter. Just as you would eliminate physical things that pile up in your home, you need to keep tabs on how you are feeling mentally, physically and spiritually at all times to avoid ending up right back where you started.

Remember that feeling tired despite good sleep habits is an early sign that your mind is cluttered. You are likely not sleeping as well as you think, and what brainpower you do have during the day is preoccupied with thoughts that don't serve you.

Do yourself a favor and take some time to check in with your thoughts every day. Are you feeling energized and clear? Is your brain foggy and sluggish? Do you feel anxious, angry or sad? Assess where you are so you can spend some time making improvements when necessary.

A great way to get in touch with your inner spirit and check in with your thoughts is to meditate. Taking just ten or fifteen minutes every day to sit and be inside your mind is a great practice. Meditation can be very simple and doesn't need to cut into your day. Set your alarm clock a few minutes early and take that time to lay in bed and simply think. If you feel you might fall asleep, physically sit up in bed, or try at another time of day.

Focus on the sound of your breath, or invest in a guided meditation soundtrack. The goal is to quickly get in touch with your inner self so that it can guide you. We all have an inner voice that helps us plan our day and our lives, but very few of us actually listen.

Some people say that exercise is a form of meditation, and to each their own. It is scientifically proven that exercise of all types helps reduce stress hormones, calms nerves and promotes emotional well-being. Of course, it also strengthens the body and the immune system as well, leading to better overall health.

Something as simple as taking a walk outside every day is enough to help clear your mind and get you thinking optimally again. If you tend to get inside your head when you are exercising, try using the activity as a dual meditation session. That is, concentrate and focus only on what you are doing. If you are out walking in the woods, take in the scenery and try to let other thoughts float to the back burner.

No matter the activity, it is important to give your mind time to rest and recover. Your brain is a sensitive organ, just like any other. It needs downtime to restore proper function. We can see the truth in this by recognizing how sluggish and foggy we are when we are running on little sleep. Downtime while awake is just as vital. Think of this downtime as an opportunity for the tiny librarians in your brain to sort through all of the open books and put them back on the shelves. Having this time to gather your thoughts makes you better able to make sense of them later.

People who are overworked often slip in their performance because they work TOO much. Yes, there is such a thing despite what some of the world's most eccentric billionaires tell you. Taking breaks and allowing for rest actually makes you a better worker, allows you to be more alert and active in your daily life, and more proactive for your future.

On that note, keeping the past in the past and the future in the future is also vital in preventing the buildup of mental clutter. The most important moment in life is the one you are living right now. The rest is history, and we cannot predict what will happen in the future. There is no sense in worrying about things we do not yet know, and worrying means you are only suffering a second time provided that it actually comes to fruition.

Instead, take a mindful stance, and concentrate on being present and active at the moment. Focus on the work that you are doing, appreciate that you are hanging out with family and friends, and do things that strike your fancy at the moment. Learn to appreciate the subtle intricacies that are life, and soak in every moment. You truly don't know when your time is up. Do you really want to go out thinking about that horrible meeting you had yesterday?

A good rule of thumb is to check in with yourself at least three times during the day. Ask yourself a few good questions: Do you remember the ins and outs of what you have done over the past few hours? Do you feel as if you have accomplished something? Do you feel content? Excited? Agitated? Truly take stock of that time and decide where to fit in some balance. If you worked hard the last few hours, maybe it's time to give your brain a quick break and do something fun and silly for a few minutes.

What can you do in the next few hours to improve yourself? Find a shred of happiness and joy? Something that will propel you into the future you have always dreamed of? You must always keep thoughts of your innermost desires close to the front of your brain. Think of them as your operating manual. Are you acting in such a way that is in line with your innermost needs and morals? What can you do to better live those dreams?

Remember that mental clutter will dissipate more and more as you get closer to living your true inner passions and dreams. The energy of the universe will flow in your favor if you just give in to what your inner self truly desires. It's what YOU want, so why are you fighting it?

CHAPTER 5:

Why Less is More in All Aspects of Life

Whether you like to believe it or not, the revolution of essentialism is occurring right now within all the chaos of the world. No, it certainly is not a political statement, but it is a lifestyle choice that requires us to choose ourselves and all the things we want to get out of the **one** life we all have to live. There are hundreds of thousands of people just like you that are choosing a more minimalist way of life. The thing is, a simpler way of living has been around for hundreds of years and has easily sufficed us just fine.

The essentialist lifestyle is gaining a lot of influence around the world, especially as the generation of millennial individuals are taking over the planet and changing our perceptions of things such as the media. A simpler life means you are to engulf yourself in the richness that every single life has to offer and introduces a better focus on what we are passionate about. It requires us to invest our time wisely on the most important things in life.

The phrase "less is more" will be one you hear quite often throughout this book as you flip through its pages. It is the core of the minimalist and essentialist lifestyle and can be applied to every single aspect of everyday life, even business. Simplifying things and bringing back the basics can make life ten times easier. In our world, there is so much complexity with the overload of information, which perpetuates a fear within us that we are "missing out."

There is a new piece of technology, a new product, and new startups that occur about every hour of every day, which means that so many of us are bogged down with hefty to-do lists, distractions, and temptations that keep us from being the best we can be and doing the best work we could do. Our society is overwhelmed, to say the least. We are taught from the get-go to desire more. Whether it be more goals, dreams, desires, possessions, information, etc. We thrive on having more people liking our posts on social media, we love when we pile more money in our bank accounts, we strive to have more things in our homes, and we tend to have too many thoughts in our mind. The list of chaos has the potential to go on and on.

But when you really take a chance to think about it, the bigger picture behind that cloud of chaos is, well, frightening. Human beings seem to be naturally wired to make life more complex than it needs to be. Thankfully, we can unlearn the behaviors that are making our lives complicated. I am sure you are excited to hear that there is a way back to a much simpler, happier way of life that engages in having a genuine peace of mind within the chaos that lies outside our front doors.

Less **is** more because of the result of the decrease of unnecessary worry and stress, as it takes away the unimportant tasks, possessions, and people in life. There is more room for contentment, meaning, focus, and freedom. These are the four things that every single person in the world desires the most, yet still, put walls up in the form of possessions and other unvital things that inhibit them from fulfilling happiness. The reality is, when we strive for less of everything, we start getting much more in return. We begin getting more things done and achieve the great results of accomplishing our goals and dreams.

As you can imagine, there are some amazing and life-changing takeaways from pursuing less in your life:

Essentialists have the power to choose

Essentialism is powerful based on the fact that we refocus our lives to having the ability to choose for ourselves what we want in life and out of life. The power of choice in how we respond, what we do, and what we think helps in the proactive fight against being reactive and helps us to prioritize our life.

We are allowing ourselves to be prioritized by outside factors, from our job, how much we make, what we choose to buy, etc. Essentialism digs deeper into ourselves to inquire and evaluates the options we pick every single day.

If not a clear 'yes,' then certainly a clear 'no'

To make the best decisions for a more focused life, essentialism teaches us to not only explore but evaluate the options we are given thoroughly before making a decision. This is one of the staple qualities of becoming an essentialist. But what about when you have several really awesome choices and the decisions to choose is not a clear one?

Eliminate everything that is not beneficial or does not provide a positive impact on your life. Learning and understanding trade-offs is another critical point of essentialism. You should not focus on what you are giving up, but rather what you wish to go "big".

Elimination of unessential to discover high points of contribution

Those that do not use the concept of essentialism in their lives think that everything on their plate is important and become stressed on how they are supposed to do it all. But in essentialism, we have a different mindset and know we have the power to choose, and pick the things that matter most.

This is where the highest points of contribution come into play. Every single person on Earth has limited attention, energy, and time to give. Essentialists think deeper about how they are to fulfill their duties to discover and fulfill what they can contribute to the world. The only way to truly discover this is to discard all of the trivial things in life that are distracting us from focusing on what is more important.

Why Essentialism and Minimalism Go Hand in Hand

I am sure you have heard about the concept of minimalism a time or two. Minimalism is very similar to essentialism as it requires one to be intentional with their actions and purpose and engages in the freedom from the passion to possess. Like essentialism, it provides freedom from too many possessions and tasks that are not fulfilling to your life.

That being said, here are more fantastic ways that, thriving in an essentialist and minimalist mindset, can change every aspect of your life and discover how living with less is actually living with much, much more!

Hidden Costs

It's no secret that things consume our lives greatly. Whether sitting on a shelf, bottled or boxed, unwrapped, or taking up precious space in our homes, these are what I like to refer to as "hidden costs." I refer to them as this because people do not realize how much work they put into the working, purchasing, and maintenance of these "things."

Our society is greatly obsessed with possessions, which is not allowing us to go after the things we desire most out of life. Minimalism and essentialism allow us to become free from these hidden traps and make us understand that material items can never genuinely take the place of human relationships. Much of the population spends so much of their precious time going after things, which is distracting them from the pursuit of true happiness.

Recover Money and Time

The concept of minimalism to most folks is just about discarding things they no longer use. But in reality, minimalists don't rid themselves of everything they own, but rather discard all of the things that are deemed unvital to their happiness and prosperity.

Essentialism ties into minimalism because it allows one to gain a deeper respect to think through habits that waste time and money and skipping out on wasteful shopping and getting rid of the things that waste their time, such as a car. No more traffic jams!

Zero Followers

Social media can be thanked for heavily contributing to the madness of the everyday world we dwell in today. Staring at our phones has quite literally become the equivalent of daydreaming.

Not only does our technology contribute to e-waste once we break or are done using our devices, we allow ourselves to become distracted by all the digital noise and allow businesses to brainwash us with the desire to purchase their items.

Obviously, in today's modern world, it is difficult to rid yourself of technology. But using technology only for work or vital personal purposes will bring to light the importance of ridding yourself from apps that distract you with notifications. Your life will change as you become more present to the moment and connect with people in real life, rather than through a screen.

Constitute Space

When you have space in your life for only the things you need and rid yourself of all the clutter, both physically and mentally, you then have ample space to breathe, live, and thrive.

I can personally attest to the fact that ridding my life of all the unnecessary possessions changed my mindset by totally carving out the need for those items. There was also less stress to have to pay for more storage, and there was essentially a peace of mind that came right along with it. You cannot buy that in any store.

Meaningful Relationships

Being more essential with your life will allow you to see the world differently which will permeate all aspects of life. Your attitude will become positive and what you have done in your physical spaces by only allowing necessity will trickle into your personal life and relationships with others as well.

You will find that you only make time for those that you truly care about. You will also begin to develop an instinct against those that only like you for their own personal gain. Just like you threw away all the unnecessary things in your life in the form of possessions, you will start doing the same with people, discarding the toxic influences in your life.

Essentialism and minimalism help you to gain a deeper understanding of the vitality of maintaining a work-and-life balance. You will start to think of "smart working" much more as you give time to your goals in your career instead of staying in the same rut. When at home, you will find that you are not addicted to your phone and can spend genuine time with family and friends.

Live Happier

As we have discussed several times already, essentialism gives you the power to create more energy, time, and space for the experiences and people that make you truly happy. You will be using less, which means being less wasteful. This concept of life is good for the entire planet!

Chapter 6:

Making time for free time

You understand the need to focus on only what really matters in your life and letting the rest go. You have learned the importance of saying no the right way and how to be fully present in the moments of your day. You are going to give 100% to everything that you do so you can live in a mindful, more authentic way. You are reclaiming your life and everyone around you will benefit. But what about you?

It cannot be stressed enough that you are also a priority. That is not selfish. This is your life and you have to take care of yourself so that you can be fully present and engaged with others. If you ignore your own needs, just like when your life was out of control then you are really not practicing essentialism. You are also shortchanging yourself. The whole point of essentialism is stripping away all the things that don't matter and focus on what does. This includes you.

In an earlier chapter, the serious repercussions of consistent stress and exhaustion were highlighted. The main reason for the existence of those dangerous levels of stress and fatigue is simple. You are doing too much and you are not giving your body and mind a chance to rest. Now that you have prioritized the essentials in life, be sure not to leave yourself off that list.

It is easy to fall back into old patterns of behavior. Especially, if you suddenly have free time that you didn't have before. That free time is for you to focus on you. It may be tempting to use it to add just one more thing to your to-do list. Resist this temptation or you will find yourself back to the point that you started from.

Guard this free time on your schedule and use it for you. You need rest and relaxation. You need time to heal physically, emotionally, and mentally. That crazy schedule that you just left behind took its toll on you as you stayed stressed and exhausted for months and years. You need time to recover from that. You won't bounce back overnight but you will see improvements in your life every day.

You prioritized the rest of your life now prioritize your free time. That may sound counterproductive. Its free time, therefore it's free and doesn't need limitations or priorities, right? Not so. The first priority that you owe to yourself about your free time is to schedule it. Make sure you have free time every day even for half an hour. It is such a vital component to your health and happiness that it is important that you always make time for it.

Next, decide what you want to do with your free time. You don't have to settle for just one focus. You can include everything and anything that you find enjoyable and relaxing on your list. After all, it's your free time, you have earned now enjoy!

If you are not sure where to get started here are a few suggestions:

- **Meditation or quiet time.** After the emotional roller coaster of the last few months and years, you may feel disconnected from yourself. Take time to practice meditation or sit quietly for at least 10 minutes a day to reconnect with yourself and recharge.

- **Yoga.** If you have eaten junk food and haven't exercised in years, you may feel sluggish and disconnected from your physical self. Practicing yoga is a great way to gently reconnect with your body and release tension.

- **Start a new hobby.** Or pick up an old one. You may have always wanted to learn carpentry or crochet. Before your life became a maelstrom you may have enjoyed painting. Take time to reconnect with your creative side and get started on a hobby.

- **Read.** If you are a reader and can't remember the last time you read a book or flipped through a magazine, then you might enjoy scheduling a few minutes each day to cuddling up with a good book or reading a magazine article.

- **Take a walk.** If you have a dog, take him with you. Go on a walk for a few minutes in the afternoon or morning. You will enjoy the exercise and it is a chance to gently reconnect with your body and get moving again.

- **Get some sleep.** Be sure to schedule a good night's sleep. Everyone is different but the recommended amount of sleep for recovery and healing is between 7 to 8 hours a night. Try to incorporate a good night's sleep every night and see how much better you will feel.

- **Watch something.** If you never had the chance to catch up on a favorite show or can't remember the last time you watched a favorite movie, then schedule it. It's important that you reconnect to yourself and sometimes you just need a good movie to do that.

- **Journal**. Did you have a diary in high school? Did you keep a journal before your life got crazy? Keeping a journal is a proven way to help yourself heal. The pages of the journal don't have to be emotionally drenched diatribes, you can also have fun. You can make lists or keep an art journal. The important thing to remember about journaling is that it is as unique as you are and it is a great way to reconnect with yourself and express emotions.

- **Put together a puzzle.** Take some time to do something fun and mentally challenging that doesn't involve work. When was the last time you put together a puzzle or completed a Crossword or Sudoku? It will give you a chance to relax and enjoy the accomplishment of solving a problem.

Now that you are adding free time back into your life, don't stop there. **Schedule something special for yourself that you can really look forward to.** Think about everything that you always wanted to do but did not have the time. It doesn't have to be grandiose; it can be simple. You can also include family and friends. You can schedule a whole day or weekend. It can be a day at the art museum or a weekend fly fishing or antiquing. Just remember to make it stress-free and fun. Go to the spa, go camping, do anything that you always wanted to just relax and enjoy every minute of it.

Free time is an important part of your life. Guard it and use it well. It is your opportunity to rest, relax and enjoy your life. It is also your chance to reconnect with the person that got pushed to the bottom of your list when you stressed and your schedule was out of control. Reconnect with who you are and you will be happier. A happier you will also mean healthier, better relationships with everyone around you.

Chapter 7:

Say goodbye to all the time vampires

Time vampire? What is that? A time vampire is not an interdimensional, time traveling, blood sucking creature of the underworld. A time vampire is anything that sucks time away from your life with little to no return on the investment. It is any activity that we engage in that is absolutely useless.

It is the time that we spend surfing the internet for hours with no real objective. It is the murky end of youtube or when you find yourself on Facebook for hours. It can be mindlessly watching reality TV shows or playing a game on your PS4 that you don't particularly care about. It's any activity that you do mindlessly that does not involve any real thinking or active participation from you.

All of these activities can be relaxing and can be enjoyed in moderation. However, when you are already exhausted and stretched paper thin, you might think that you are doing these actions as a form of downtime but in reality, they have become escapism. You are literally wasting hours of your week or month on the internet and watching TV and they don't really matter.

Can you imagine what you could do with some of that time given back to you? You could actually get some sleep, relax and watch something you really care about not just whatever happens to be on. You could spend an extra 20 minutes in the evening with your spouse and children. You could walk around the block a few times and get some exercise. You could take up knitting or read a chapter in that book that you meant to finish. There is no limit to what you could do with that time given back to you.

Essentialism is not just about stripping all the nonessentials from your work and personal life, it also about cleaning the clutter out of your everyday life. This clutter is full of the time vampires. It's late and you have just put the kids to bed, you have a few minutes and you decide to check in on Facebook. An hour later, you are still on Facebook doing nothing productive.

Where did that hour go? Then you realize that you have been the victim of a time vampire.

If you look at your life and your everyday activities you will realize that there are lots of ways that you can moderate the amount of time that you spend on time vampires.

You just have to be vigilant with your time until you develop better habits about certain activities. You can still have fun and occasionally go on an internet surfing binge, just don't do it all the time, especially when you could be doing something healthier and better for your life. If you are already super busy and your schedule is bursting at the seams, then that extra 30 minutes that you just spent streaming a TV show that you won't remember in 6 months is definitely a waste of your precious time. And you can never get those 30 minutes back. Poof! Like magic, it's gone.

Rather than mourn its loss, you can do something way more productive. You can start viewing your daily activities with a more discerning eye. Don't do anything reckless such as canceling your phone service or turning off your internet connection. You may need both, but do start thinking about what you are doing with them. In an earlier chapter, the first step in essentialism was to prioritize what you really wanted to get out of your life and what you wanted to focus your energy and passion on. Now, it is time to prioritize the daily activities that are robbing you of your time.

This is a list of questions that you can start with:

- How much time do you spend on the internet a day checking in on Facebook and spending time on youtube?

- How much time do you spend texting friends and family, even coworkers?

- Social media? How much time are you wasting on social media?

- How much time do you spend mindlessly watching television? In particular, shows that you aren't really into, they just happen to be on?

- If you are a gamer, how much time are you wasting on ordinary games just to take your mind off your day?

Once you have examined your day to day life for the obvious and not so obvious time vampires, you need to take a few steps to prevent these activities from taking over the downtime that you have worked so hard to gain. There are many ways that you can take control of this part of your life.

Here are a few suggestions and tips:

- **Set a timer.** When you are on the internet and plan to indulge in a time-wasting internet surfing, be sure to set a time. You really don't have to set a timer. Just keep an eye on the time and set a time a limit for how long you will be on the computer. Then stick to it.

- **Limit your texting.** When you are with your family or at dinner with your spouse, put the phone away (unless you are expecting an urgent text or call). You can always check your texts after dinner. Spending time texting back and forth with a coworker over a subject that honestly could have waited until work the next day is a waste of your time.

- **Social media and Facebook.** These two are monumental time vampires. It is easy to think to yourself that you are just going to check in or see what's going on. Naturally, a few minutes can turn into an hour and before you know it you are deeply involved in a Facebook conversation about politics with some guy that is a friend of your ex-college roommate.

- **Limit how much television and internet shows that you watch.** If you are deeply into a television show, then put on your comfy clothes, get a delicious beverage and relax on your couch with the latest episode. Enjoy. You have worked hard and you deserve a break. Just don't let it become an everyday habit or your new go-to activity for late nights.

Now that you see all the time vampires that are lurking in your life and robbing your day of precious minutes, you can do something about them. There are times when you need a few pleasant minutes of distraction, just try not to let these minutes turn into hours. Make a list of everything that you do during the day that can be modified and moderated. Prioritize those activities and think of this as a tradeoff. You are giving up an hour of Facebook every day for an hour of sleep, or an hour having dinner with your family. By moderating the time vampires in your everyday life, you will be able to successfully find more time to devote to the essentials in your life.

Chapter 8:

Giving 100%

Imagine what you could achieve in your life if you gave 100%? What dreams could you make into reality or goals could you attain? With a schedule so jam-packed full of obligations and responsibilities, you are probably finding it difficult to be good at anything. You can never be really good at something until you give it your all, not what you can spare.

If you are spread so thin over your life that you feel like you are only able to give anything part of the attention that it deserves then you are ready to make a change. Change can be scary but ultimately it will be better for you. Once you decide what stays in your life and what needs to go then you can start really concentrating on making the things that you decided to keep truly great.

You may love your job but feel overwhelmed by all of your other responsibilities. You may find yourself going in at the last minute or even late because you are exhausted. Being already tired first thing in the morning with a whole day ahead of you is no way to build a successful career. You will be more prone to making mistakes and your work will be inconsistent and suffer. This is especially true if you have a very demanding career. Pressure, stress, and exhaustion are never a great combination for upward mobility in most companies.

If you practically despise your job and have decided to make pursuing your dream job one of your priorities then you will definitely need as much rest as you can get. Chasing a dream and building a small business or learning a new trade takes mental strength and discipline. You will spend long hours working hard with very little reward until your new job really takes off or your new business gets out of the red. You will need to completely focus your attention and put your heart and passion into your work. This is not something that you can do halfway. Your success will depend on your own hard work. You have to be prepared to give it your all.

Career and dream jobs may not be your ultimate goal. Imagine that you have a lifelong dream to sail around the world or buy a house in the mountains and retire early. If you are not able to fully devote your attention and energy to pursuing this dream then how are you ever going to make it happen? So many people talk about what they are going to do one day. Don't be content with one day, start thinking about how you are going to make it happen now or in the very near future. A Dream like that requires your full attention and a plan to make it happen. When you get to the essentials in your life you will be able to make the dream a reality.

Your relationships with you friends and family are also not something that you can take for granted and devote only part of your attention to. The love and tenderness that you feel with your loved ones is something that needs to be nurtured. You want to be present and give your all to these relationships. Being present and really taking an interest in a friend's conversation or your spouse's day at work can make all the difference in the world in a relationship.

Work, chasing a dream, family and friends are all priorities that you can fully focus on when you have stripped the nonessentials away from your life and are now focusing on the essentials, only. You will be amazed at what you can accomplish when you put your blood, sweat, and tears into something. Giving 100% will mean leaving something else with 0. That is the choice that you will have to make. Essentialism is not a way to carry on doing way too much and trying to make everything work. It is figuring out what you have in your life that you don't care to pursue or that you really don't want to do.

There may be choices that you have to make that may appear to be sacrifices at first glance. If you want to get the beach house one day but hate working 60 hours a week to do it, then you may have to give up something else like buying an expensive car every other year or shopping at the high-end retail stores. This would mean finding a position that is only 40 hours a week that may pay less. You can still get the beach house and keep working; you just may not be able to afford a BMW. A trade off like that would be a worthy compromise because you have identified your real essential which is the beach house and your next essential which is not having to spend so much time away from home at work. The tradeoff was the thing that you really didn't care about, the expensive car.

Essentialism works exactly like that. Devote 100% of your energy to what you have decided is important in your life and leave the rest behind.

You may find that when you prioritize your essentials that you have spent far too much time saying yes to people and projects that you really don't care about. You may have felt obligated to take them on despite the fact that deep down you knew that you could not really handle it. When you have decided on what is essential for you, you may have to change your behavior and that may shake some people up. If you have always said yes to every extra time-consuming project that your boss asked you to do, she may be taken aback slightly by the fact that you say no. Your coworkers may not understand when you tell them that you can't make that 7-layer chocolate cake for every company party and instead will be bringing cookies from the bakery. These people will eventually get over it. You have to be happy with your life and understand that you are not obligated to make these other people happy all the time.

Just be prepared to make the difficult choices. Once you have decided to devote all of your energy towards making something truly wonderful and successful then the tough choices will feel well worth it. You may even feel like a weight has been lifted off of your shoulders when you decide to stop trying to do everything. You can actually smile and laugh and once in a while sleep late.

Chapter 9:

Reframe ALL Negative Thoughts

Our thinking processes are necessary for survival and for competing in a modern world. Critical thinking gives us the ability to solve problems quickly and effectively. Creative thinking allows us to develop original, diverse, and elaborate ideas and connections. But it's the uninvited negative thinking that clutters our minds and often drains our enthusiasm for life.

According to Australian psychologist Dr. Russ Harris, author of **The Happiness Trap: How to Stop Struggling and Start Living,** "Thus, evolution has shaped our brains so that we are hardwired to suffer psychologically: to compare, evaluate, and criticize ourselves, to focus on what we're lacking, to rapidly become dissatisfied with what we have, and to imagine all sorts of frightening scenarios, most of which will never happen. No wonder humans find it hard to be happy!"

Many people go through their entire lives victimized by their negative thoughts. They feel they have no control of what thoughts take up residence in their brains—and worse, they believe the "voices" in their heads that tell them the sky is falling.

While the negativity bias is real, it isn't impervious to your efforts for change and self-awareness. Though it may feel natural to allow your mind to wander into worry and despair, you've reinforced negative thinking by not challenging it, and by accepting your thoughts as your identity. But you have the power to recognize this tendency and change it by **building the reframing habit**.

The first step is to notice your thought patterns and interrupt them before they get out of control.

Here are six strategies you can use throughout your day to break the pattern and begin taming your mind.

Each of these strategies takes just a few minutes to employ.

Strategy 1. Be the Watcher

Start by becoming aware of your thoughts. Separate your "self" from your thoughts, and just observe what is going on in your mind.

The trick here is to do this in an impartial manner where you're **not** judging any particular thought. Simply be conscious of yourself as a detached witness to your thoughts.

This exercise can be done sporadically throughout the day **or** during a meditation session. Observing your thoughts rather than attaching to them disempowers the thoughts and the emotions they foster.

Strategy 2. Name That Thought

Another way to separate yourself from your thoughts is by mentally acknowledging that they are nothing more than thoughts—**not** your reality.

For example, if you think, **"I'll never get all of this done,"** change the mental dialog to **"I'm having the thought that I'll never get all of this done."**

This reinforces the fact that you are not your thoughts.

Strategy 3. Just Say No

When you catch yourself in mental looping or worry, simply say, "STOP!" out loud (vocalizing reinforces the interruption), and then visualize a heavy metal wall slamming down in front of your runaway thoughts.

Barrie sometimes visualizes pushing negative thoughts into a deep hole or putting them into a balloon that floats away.

Strategy 4. Try the Rubber Band Trick

Wear a rubber band on your wrist. Whenever you see it, stop and notice your thoughts. If you are stuck in negative thinking, put the rubber band on the other wrist or gently pop it on your wrist. This physical action interrupts the flow of negative thought.

Strategy 5. Know Your Triggers

Often, overthinking and negativity are triggered by a person, situation, or physical state. Pay attention to common worries and anxieties you brood about.

Is there anything that happens that sets these off in your mind?

If so, write down the triggers so you're aware when they happen. This awareness can help prevent you from being ambushed by negative thoughts.

Strategy 6. Distract Yourself

Break the cycle using distraction. Do something that will occupy your mind so there's no room for the negative thoughts. Immerse yourself in a project that involves focus and brainpower.

If you're stuck in the car or waiting in line, go through the multiplication tables in your head or try to memorize a poem.

Chapter 10:

Living in the Present Moment

Have you noticed that your thoughts oscillate between your past and the future? This is the way of nature. You never live in the present. Your thoughts wander. You are reminded of an experience, and abruptly you feel sad. All of a sudden, your thoughts swing into the future, and you are filled with dread and anxiety. This is your usual state of mind. Your mind is filled with thoughts all the time, and there is no room left to do something productive.

Mindfulness techniques have become quite popular nowadays, and you hear about them all the time. Some aspects of mindfulness are extremely powerful in decluttering the mind. Living in the present moment is one such benefit which you must understand.

Your past is surely full of experiences, both good and bad. These memories are a product of your mind. They may be real or simply imaginary. It depends on your perspective, but they interfere with your present ability to be productive. You are distracted and worse; your decisions are colored by your memories. In a way, you are a prisoner of your memories. Old memories take up space and fill your mind. There are clutter and chaos. Unless you remove old memories from your mind, you cannot move forward.

The thoughts about your future are worse. Your mind connects your old memories and projects them into the future. You are filled with dread and anxiety, thinking about all the things which are likely to go wrong. You feel that nothing will go as per plan, and surprisingly you encounter problems though they are not the same as you had imagined. What do you think will happen when you are in such a state of mind?

Now, imagine yourself in a perfect mindful state, in which your mind is focused on the present. Your worries and apprehensions about the past and future will no longer clutter your ability to think. You will be more productive, and your life will be free of restraints.

Better said than done, you will say. Living in the present moment is not as easy as it looks. You need much more than focus to achieve mindfulness. Decluttering your mind means removing certain traits from your personality. You are born with certain innate behavioral traits – fear, anger, passion, possessiveness, and greed. These instinctive responses were indeed critical to survival once upon a time. You must fear a lion otherwise you will be eaten by it. Anger is a powerful survival instinct. But these traits, which were once useful, have become an impediment to success. There are no lions in our life, but many of us continue to behave like a gorilla. We get into a rage and verbal duels though they are unproductive and destructive emotions.

Mindfulness means becoming conscious of our place in the scheme of things. Here, there is no scope for exhibiting anger and greed. There is plenty of everything. You have to get out of scarcity mentality and get into the mindset of plenty. You will find fewer negative or fearful thoughts during your meditation practice which we have discussed earlier. The fog of anger and greed distorts your vision. You are unable to see beyond the immediate results. Clear your mind from these primordial emotions and don't give an excuse that you are human and therefore bound to get angry. These destructive emotions are best left in history or anthropological books.

Your fear of failure stops you from achieving real success in life. You don't take that bold decision because you are afraid of failure. Your mind is filled with negative consequences of your actions. Why are you fearful of the future? You are afraid because of your expectations. Remove expectations, and your mind will be able to think freely. You will be more creative. You will be bold. You will no longer be afraid because the thought of success or failure no longer weighs on your mind. This decluttering of your mind from fearful consequences of your actions is the key to success.

Mindfulness takes you to a different level of existence. You become aware of your environment, you reflect on your thoughts and actions, and as a result, you act in an appropriate manner.

Chapter 11:

Looking into The Mirror

Imagine you are driving in your car on a dirt road. Your vision is not clear because of the dust, and you put all your effort in driving. As a result, you don't enjoy the journey. You are forever fighting the dust and trying to look beyond it. This is exactly what happens when your mind is cluttered. You spend all your time trying to look through the fog of confusion. You even forget about the destination because you are doing all you can to simply remain on the road. The point is this – you can't avoid driving down the dusty road. This is life. Modern life is full of anxiety, tension, and pressure. You have to navigate your life through it. How do you look beyond this turmoil and find peace?

The solution is simple. There are some meditation techniques which allow you to filter out the noise and dust swirling around your mind. These are not do-once and forget type of practices. You have to regularly practice meditation to derive maximum benefit from it. Just like you eat and sleep every day, you must also meditate on a daily basis.

Follow these simple instructions for the next ten to fifteen minutes.

Find a noise free place in your home and sit down comfortably. You can either sit down on the floor with crossed legs or in a chair with a straight back. You must ensure that your posture is straight with backbone held erect with the support of the chair if required. Your body should be relaxed with the palm of both your hands held on your thigh. Hold your head high and gently close your eyes.

Take a deep breath. Feel your breath flowing through your nose. The air is cool when entering your nostrils. Hold your breath for a few moments. Now exhale slowly. The air going out of your nostrils is warm. Let go of your mind. Inhale and exhale ten times.

You will experience calm and serenity in your mind. Your breath has the power to affect your mood. You would have noticed that you begin to breathe heavily when you are angry. Deep and prolonged breath relaxes your mind.

Pay attention to the sounds around you. Listen to sounds which are coming from near and slowly let your ears experience sounds from far away. Do not associate any experience with a sound. Do not react to any sound. You are simply an observer, a witness to the sound. Experience the sounds around you for two minutes.

Bring your mind to your thoughts. You may have good thoughts or bad thoughts, sad or happy thoughts, sexual or spiritual thoughts, desirable or undesirable thoughts. Your mind is never free of thoughts. Let the thoughts flow. Do not intervene. Do not stop the flow of thoughts. Simply observe the thoughts. These thoughts are nothing but a reflection of yourself. These thoughts are not coming from somewhere else. You are these thoughts. There is no need to feel proud or ashamed of your thoughts. Let it be. This exercise is pretty simple. Observe your thoughts for a few minutes as an observer and witness.

Discontinue the free flow of thoughts. Now, intentionally bring a good, happy thought in your mind. Fetching a good thought is easy.

Observe the thought and reflect on it for some moments and let it go. Repeat a few times.

Now, bring a bad thought to your mind. Observe the bad thoughts and let it go. Repeat a few times.

Get a good and bad thought alternatively into your mind and let them go. Repeat a few times.

The total time spent in this meditation can vary from ten to fifteen minutes depending on your experience. You will feel total calm and relaxation of the mind after completing this practice.

You will notice that it is quite easy to remove good thoughts from the mind. It is the bad thoughts, negative thoughts and fearful thoughts which are difficult to get rid of. Slowly, after a few days or weeks, you will be able to consciously bring thoughts into your mind, reflect on it and remove from your mind effortlessly. Your mind will become free of unnecessary thoughts, and you will be able to think clearly. Your focus will improve tremendously. You will become more productive and super-efficient. Don't be surprised if your friends, colleagues and family comment on your new found energy. This meditation technique can change your life dramatically. You must practice meditation daily but do not pressurize yourself into it. It should be voluntary and pleasurable. Some people experience the positive results within weeks while others may take some months to feel the difference.

Your mind needs spring cleaning, just like your home or office. All kinds of thoughts fill your mind. Some are constructive while others are detrimental. You must declutter your mind daily with this meditation technique. Most successful people practice some meditation to refresh their mind. They may do it consciously or unconsciously. But the benefits are real and palpable. Meditate regularly, and you will see your life change right in front of your eyes.

Chapter 12:

The Magic of Positive Attitude

Meditation and creative visualization may work wonderfully when you are sitting in a silent place, but things change dramatically when you are thrown into the busyness of life. Getting jolted by the commuters in a Metro can shake you out of your meditative state of mind. The clutter seems to pile up suddenly and ominously, and you are overwhelmed. You should have powerful tools which will clear the clutter as and when they start occupying your mind. Positive attitude provides a powerful means to handle the daily heap of debilitating emotions which collects in your mind.

Let's go back to the basics. Your boss, like everyone else's, can be the major source of irritation. Bosses have the power to freeze and shut out your brain. They can quick and efficiently clutter things up. What do you think would be a strong antidote to this clutter-machine? Positive attitude in this context would mean acceptance. Instead of fighting the inevitable, you must accept the people and situations as they are. When you do this, you are free from the anxiety and tension which you would normally feel. The excess baggage of emotions can be easily discarded if you accept that your boss will behave today as he has behaved earlier. This is a compelling concept which can relieve you of your burden of expectations. Like you remove thoughts from your mind during meditation you must remove the bad experience with your boss. Imagine that you are simply an observer, a witness to the interaction between your boss and your physical self. Your mind will immediately release all the toxic thoughts building up in your mind.

You must observe all events during the day from the position of a witness. The negativity which arises due to your involvement will automatically vanish, and you will maintain a calm demeanor. Distancing yourself from your experiences gives you the power to be truly calm and peaceful.

Your reality is created by your mind. The world looks exactly the way you imagine it to be. Your mind and thoughts have the power to create your future. You feel insecure and timid when you add negativity to your thoughts. Separate this negativity and you are left with pure joy. You are already on your way towards this decluttering process. A positive attitude allows you to handle the day to day frustrations and worries and does not allow negativity to accumulate in your mind. Imagine that you bring old furniture and stuff every day and dump them in your living room. What do you think will happen? Your living room will have no space left, and you may be forced to start storing them in another room. Unfortunately, you can't add another room in your mind. You have only one room for memories, and you have to make do with it. Ideally, you won't have to declutter your mind because you just didn't fill it up in the first place. You cleaned your mind every day and kept your living room spotless and clean.

It's never too late to start cleaning up your mind. Decluttering is a two-step process. You remove old, useless memories from your mind using the techniques explained in this book. Simultaneously you must not allow new garbage to accumulate by practicing a positive attitude.

Over some weeks or months, your mind will be pristine and back to its original creative self. This state of mind is also called bliss. You start enjoying your life to the full. You look at the world with new enthusiasm. You become an explorer by escaping from the prison of conditioning which was imposed on you. A positive attitude does not mean you won't face problems. The only difference is that you will now look at problems as opportunities. This subtle change in mental frame of reference has the power to transform your life completely.

Chapter 13:

The Psychology of Clutter

If any of the costs of clutter discussed in the above section resonate with you, then you may want to declutter your space and stop paying those prices. Before you can create a plan for ongoing organization and declutter, you need to understand some things about the psychology of clutter. Understanding the thought processes that lead to clutter will help you stop it from occurring over and over again. After all, clearing away the mess only to allow it to increase again meets Einstein's definition of insanity.

Why We Keep Things

Physical clutter arises because we keep items in our homes or offices. One of the key aspects of conquering clutter is to understand why you keep the things you do. Generally, we keep extra or unneeded items around because we believe we might need them in the future; we have a sentimental attachment to them or we perceive a value in the object that makes it hard to throw away.

Monetary Value

If you paid good money for an item, you may find it difficult to throw away, even if you know you have no use for it. In cases like this, it is best to give the item to a friend, donate it for a tax break or sell it online or in a yard sale. It is much easier to part with such items when you are receiving some sort of value in return.

Sentimental Collections

There are some things that are simply irreplaceable due to sentimental value. Old pictures capture favorite memories, family heirlooms harken back to our history and small mementos remind us of great events. It can be hard to get rid of sentimental items, so you may want to consider a more organized storage option. Pictures can be scanned into the computer and stored on an external hard drive. Not only will this reduce clutter, it will also preserve your memories safely.

Collections and heirlooms can be kept in well-organized cabinets or spaced throughout the home as tasteful decorations. Remember what I said about my husband's aunt? Because she is organized, her collections do not actually create clutter.

When keeping things for their sentimental value, you do need to ensure that they are irreplaceable and really evoke personal emotions. Plastic souvenirs from your latest beach trip might not make the cut, but a small memento from your honeymoon is often worth keeping.

A Possible Future Need

It is amazing what we keep because we might need it in the future. My husband keeps all sorts of cardboard boxes and containers. He might need to store something or ship something. I have a problem with hanging on to bits and pieces of craft supplies. I will keep a tiny ball of yarn because I might incorporate it into a future crochet project. It matters very little that I rarely have time to crochet anymore or that I do not like the color. I perceive a possible future use, so I am hard pressed to toss out an otherwise useless item. In our basement at this moment, we have several half-used cans of house paint, a stack of old carpet squares and a few odd bits of plywood. We have no plans for using these items in the immediate future, but we still hold onto them.

The trick with evaluating items like this is that you very well might have a use for them in the future. It would be a shame to toss out perfectly good and costly wood, and then realize you want to build a shelf. My husband's family tells a story of how his father got so tired of the craft supply collection in their home that he went on a cleaning spree. As he swept random paper and other items into the garbage, he inadvertently tossed out a pair of real diamond earrings. They also tell a story about how my father-in-law hid all his baseball cards in a special location in his boyhood home. Years later his mother threw out a box of mint-condition and valuable cards because they looked like junk to her.

It takes a well-disciplined mind to evaluate items in the clutter pile to determine if they truly have a future value or use. To keep yourself from going to either extreme, carefully consider each item with others in your home. Ask these questions:

- Is there a concrete plan to use the item within the next six to twelve months?

- Is the item in good working order?

- Is the item of significant monetary value?

If you can answer yes to at least two of the above questions, then the item may be worth storing. Otherwise, you should strongly consider getting rid of it. There are ways to decrease the struggle it takes to get rid of an item. I reduced most of my yarn stash by giving it to a young lady who was learning to crochet. She was delighted with the abundant yarn choice and quickly put almost all of it to use.

Chapter 14:

Accessing your Subconscious

The key to success in life lies in the subconscious. You carry out certain activities automatically because your subconscious dictates your actions. You don't think most of the time consciously. Your actions are not deliberate. The subconscious is a factory where all your thoughts are collected and then transformed into reality. The process is complex, and the subconscious is likely to get confused when confronted by a wave of thoughts. Creating meaning from the meaningless jumble of thoughts is fraught with danger. The subconscious has to work through the clutter and arrive at some conclusion. More the clutter tougher is the task of your subconscious to find meaning.

Clutter, in other words, is stagnant energy residing in your subconscious. This pool of energy is stuck in your mind and has to be released to unleash its power. This energy is like a coiled snake which is waiting to strike but is dormant in most of us. There are many ways to access this coiled energy. Creative visualization is one technique to release this coiled energy.

Decluttering the mind and finding the meaning of life should not be directly compared with physical clutter. This is a mistake which you are likely to make. The main difference is that mental clutter is hidden deep within the recess of your mind. You can't simply take a broom and clean the cobwebs in your mind because the cobwebs are invisible. The clutter in your mind moreover a result of an overactive brain instead of a lifeless body. You overthink, and all these thoughts choke, clog and block your decision-making processes. The clutter accumulates over years and years. The older you get, the weight of your thoughts becomes more. Accessing the inner core of your mind needs practice and knowledge of the process. You have already read and hopefully practiced the techniques explained earlier. Let's now see how you can use creative visualization to access your subconscious.

The first requirement for creative visualization is calmness of mind. You can't be frantic and desperate about anything. In such a state of mind, you will only create further problems. As you learned earlier, your mind is a cauldron in which your thoughts keep brewing new fantasies. They are fear, anger combined with chunks of joy and expectation. There is hope as well as hopelessness. By regular meditation practice, you can gradually attain a calm state of mind. Just after meditation practice is the best time to begin creative visualization.

Your mind is blank. You don't have any thoughts, good or bad. You are experiencing inner silence. This state is ideal because you can now draw anything in this blank space. In normal life you are inhibited from thinking big, to think of the impossible because your mind is cluttered with unnecessary logic and rationality. Inhibitions kill your creativity. In a meditative state, you can draw a truly colorful picture on a large canvass of your mind.

The process of visualization must be systematic and methodical. We are pulled in different directions in our daily lives. Our thoughts wander, and our mind is disturbed. This clutters out thinking. The first step, therefore, is to decide your objective and goal. Here we are not talking about your lifetime objective which can be overwhelming in the beginning. You can begin with your career goals for instance. For example, what do you want to become or where do you wish to be in five years' time? This should be the starting point of your visualization.

Imagine that you are creating your career portrait. Once you have the outline, you can fill in the details. As you visualize your future career, you must etch out the finer details – colors, shapes, curves, depth, and tone. Your thoughts must be vivid like a living dream. As you go deeper into your visualization, become a part of it. Act like you are living through the experience.

You should not force yourself to visualize. You have a plan, but you are not rigid. You have the contours but not the final form. Be prepared to express your innermost desires without inhibition, yet not push these thoughts forcefully. It may happen that in your creative visualization practice you may drift into an unknown territory – something you were unprepared for. You must let your mind explore uncharted territory. Remember that you are not executing anything concrete. Nothing is going to happen immediately. Creative visualization fails because we want too much to happen too quickly. Unknown to us we inject urgency in our thoughts which spoils the entire visualization process.

Let the thoughts emerge spontaneously in your mind. Think about the thoughts, examine the thoughts and slowly build on these thoughts. This is the time when your subconscious is interacting with your conscious thoughts. Your subconscious is feeding your thoughts, and simultaneously it is fed by the thoughts. In this state, you are neither fully conscious nor asleep. You are not dreaming because you are aware of your thoughts. Creative visualization should last about ten minutes daily. Develop a routine in which your meditation practice is followed by creative visualization. Do not expect instant results. The combined practice will slowly dissolve the clutter in your mind, and slowly you will discover the positive effects. You can't dig through the clutter in a hurry. There is no shortcut, but the process which has been described here will certainly direct your life to spectacular success.

Chapter 15:

Have A Clearer Head

Minimalism helps to clear the mind in many ways. Firstly, it's about the physical once more. The less 'stuff' you have sitting around, the clearer you will feel. For instance, when you are at work, if you work within a desk area, do you find it easy to work when there are countless pieces of paper, folders, files, and other pieces of junk lying around? No! You can't move for things and they're taking up important space which you need for the job at hand. This is exactly the same process in your brain. The more clutter you have around you, the harder it is to focus.

There is a reason that many workplaces are streamlining their workstations - because many studies have shown that tidy desks create a tidy mind and increase productivity as a result. You can adopt the same way of thinking to any part of your life. For instance, if your car is constantly messy, full of junk, will you enjoy driving in it?

It won't be the same, that's for sure. On the other hand, if you clear everything out, throw away the junk and keep it tidy, you'll enjoy your journeys and you'll be more proud of your vehicle.

Constantly trying to keep up with everyone by owning the latest gadgets and trends creates a cluttered mind also. You're never satisfied, you're never in the moment, and you're always thinking ahead, never really content with where you are. Minimalism will teach you that a clear and tidy space will give you a clearer mind and therefore you can use that to reach your full potential in life. You will have a better basis on which to build your career, explore your likes and dislikes, etc.

Time and Space to Focus on Health, Hobbies, and Learning

A clearer headspace also gives you the time you need to focus on other things in life, e.g. your health, your hobbies, and lifelong learning. Most of us become so stuck on materialism that it takes over everything else in life. Is owning material items more important than your health?

Is owning material items more important than enjoying your spare time? Is it more important than learning new skills which could catapult your life to the next level?

By clearing out your mind and your physical space, you are creating time, something which most of us don't have enough of. You can find the things you need, you can move around much more freely, and your mind isn't cluttered. This means that you can focus on whatever it is that you want to focus on, without anything else getting in the way.

You will feel lighter on your feet and that will directly affect your health. You won't be dumbed down by the need to own, and you won't be as stressed out as a result. Remember, owning material goods is an expensive business, and money worries can become so serious that they create a world of stress and anxiety. None of that is positive.

When you feel less stressed and healthier on the inside, you are more likely to think about effective and fun ways to fill your time. You can create new hobbies, perhaps walking, something active, or something creative, and you can learn new things too. You'll have the time and space to think about your life and what you want from it, and if that means going back to school and learning a language or something new altogether, go for it! Minimalism will give you the confidence to go for what you want because you have realized what is truly important in life.

Less Focus on Material Possessions and Competition

When you focus on always being ahead of everyone else, e.g. trying to be the one with the latest gadget, for instance, you'll always be stressed and you'll never be still. As we mentioned earlier in our book, technology and fashions move at such an alarming rate, it's impossible to always be the one with the best stuff. A phone is never the latest model for long! This means that you're constantly on the lookout for the latest thing, you're always trying to have the cash to actually purchase these things, many of which are extremely expensive.

Being in competition with everyone else, i.e. wanting to be the one who has the latest things, is exhausting. It doesn't allow you to form meaningful relationships with anyone. How can you be a true friend to someone if you're always striving to prove that you're better than them?

Having less focus on owning material possessions and competing to be the best will allow you to be a better friend, a better family member, and a better everything to someone else. You're focused on them as a person, and not always trying to be the better one out of the two of you. Materialism is a really negative trait, and whilst it is never intended to be, it can actually ruin relationships and cause huge yawning gaps between people who were once close.

A Greater Sense of Happiness, Confidence, and Contentment

All of this adds up to one thing - happiness. When you feel lighter, you feel healthier, you're focused on the things you enjoy, and you have meaningful relationships with those around you then how can you be unhappy? You'll be more content because you are happy with what you have, you don't need to always be striving for something which you're never going to achieve or own, and you'll feel more confident in yourself as a result.

Most of us don't know what true happiness really feels like. We think we do, but we often think that happiness is when our new cellphone has been delivered from the phone company and we have a full day to play with it. That's not happiness at its deepest level, that's just a quick hit of adrenaline from owning something new. The shine quickly fades and we're looking for the next thing we can own. The highs and lows which come from this do not equate to happiness, they equate to drama and stress.

Feeling at ease with everything and not particularly needing to strive for anything that you can't reach is a truly magnificent feeling, and it can be achieved by adopting a minimalist lifestyle. The confidence which comes from feeling content and happy will actually be a major turning point in your life. When you're confident, you seek out opportunities for change, because your newly positive attitude attracts them. When they come, you're more likely to take them, and who knows where that could lead!

For instance, perhaps a promotion opportunity occurs at work and you want to go for it, but you're so stressed out living the materialistic lifestyle, running from one thing to another and never really grabbing what you want, that you don't have the confidence or sense of self-worth to go for it. On the other hand, someone who is content and happy with their lot will have the mindset of 'what have I got to lose?'. From there, wonderful things happen, usually quite unexpected things.

Chapter 16:

What about Today?

You know that your life is hectic and crazy. You are probably exhausted and stressed all the time. You know that your work life is stressful and your personal life is hanging on by a thread. Your house is a mess and you can't remember the last time you did anything fun. You somehow took the time to read this book looking for answers and advice. Hopefully, you found what you were looking for.

Now that you read the book, what is the next step? That answer is simple. Breathe. Just take a moment to breathe and take it all in. Your mind is probably racing with possibilities and questions. Can I really take my life back? What will happen when I start saying no? Can I actually make time to sleep? You have a lot to think about and consider, just don't get overwhelmed. You are already overwhelmed enough in your life, don't let this book add to it.

Today all you have to do to get the ball rolling is take 5 minutes and make a list or scribble a note. You don't have to concentrate or put too much thought into it, just write from the heart. Consider these questions. What makes you happy? If you suddenly were wealthy, what would you spend your life doing? What do you miss?

You don't have to answer these questions all in the same 5 minutes. You can spread them out. Just consider them suggestions to help you start to prioritize. Your answers that are not overly analyzed and that come from your heart are the real answers. Be honest. Be true to yourself. Ask yourself these questions and write the first thing that pops into your mind. Don't edit or change the answer. Write it down exactly as it appears in your mind. That is your truth.

Take time to think about your answers. Those answers will guide you when you sit down and spend time prioritizing your entire life. These answers will be your guideposts. Today is not about planning the rest of your life, you will get to that point when you prioritize. Today is about accepting the fact that you don't have to live like this anymore. You can change your life and you can be happy. You don't have to be exhausted and overwhelmed all the time.

Not trying to sound cliché, but today really is the first day of the rest of your life. What you are doing today will have a huge positive impact on the rest of your life. The 5 minutes that you spent may be the most important 5 minutes that you have spent in months. The answers that you wrote down are what really matters to you. Those answers are your essentials in their rawest, most pure form.

You now know what is important to you and not what you feel like you have to do, or what society tells you is supposed to be a priority to you. You have the answers scribbled hastily on a piece of paper or typed into your phone. Now that you know, it is entirely up to you to do something positive with this information.

The power to change is in your hands. There may be some tough decisions ahead and you may have to tell people no. You may have to make some changes in your finances to accommodate your dreams and your new focus on your essentials, but it will be worth it.

Everything that you give up or let go of will make room for the projects, goals, dreams, and people that really matter. You have tried to accommodate everything and everyone for far too long. Now it is time to focus on what you want to keep in your life. Now is the time to concentrate on your dreams and building great relationships with your loved ones. Now is the time to strip away all of the non-essentials from your schedule and your life and pour your energy and passion into only the essentials. Now is the time, and today is the day.

Today is so much more than 5 minutes spent answering a question. Today is the day that you commit to taking those answers and turning them into your reality. Today you actually found out what is essential in your life. What you do today and the next day and the next day after that will change your life. You now know what is essential in your life. Today is the most important step you will ever take. Make today the day that you decide that you are going to take back your life. It all starts with today.

Chapter 17:

Mindfulness Meditation

While it comes with a wide variety of additional mental and physical benefits, at its core mindfulness meditation is all about striving to become as connected to the moment as possible in hopes of bringing additional clarity and focus to your mind as a result. Mindfulness meditation is extremely simple to learn, though difficult to master, and can be done virtually anywhere and at any time. What's more, it can be used to help you remove all types of existing mental clutter, while also helping prevent new clutter from forming in the future.

To give it a try, all you need to do is focus on taking long, deep breaths and trying to take in as much of the information that your senses are providing you with as possible. While it sounds simple when written out, odds are you found it more difficult to clear your mind of outside thoughts than you anticipated. Nevertheless, making a habit out of practicing it for as little as 15 minutes a day can not only help you with your mental clutter, but also aid you when it comes to improving your overall sense of self. Mindfulness meditation will also reduce your overall levels of stress.

When it comes to practicing mindfulness meditation successfully, it is crucial that you avoid making the mistake of giving every stray thought that comes to your mind the power to derail the meditative process. To prevent this from happening, you may find it helpful to visualize all of your thoughts passing through you, each encased in its own bubble. Instead of interacting with each new thought that floats into your mind, simply watch it float by without doing more than acknowledging its existence. You may also find it useful to visualize your thoughts as the flow of water out of a faucet that you have the power to turn off.

The following is a step-by-step guide to mindfulness meditation.

Step 1: Make time

A famous mindfulness saying states that if you have the time, you should practice being mindful for 15 minutes a day; however, if you don't have time, then you should practice for 30 minutes per day. This is to say that the more hectic your life is the more benefit you can find in mindfulness mediation and why it is so crucial that you fit it into your schedule and never waver. This will become easier after you get the hang of things as you can practice being mindful virtually anywhere.

For starters, however, it is best to set aside some time each day to find a quiet place where you won't be bothered for at least 15 minutes. As with any new habit, it is important to stick with it regularly for at least 30 days if you really want to make it a part of your routine. Since it is a low-impact practice and nothing external is required, this makes it easy to fit into a busy schedule but it also makes it easy to put off until later too. You will need to consider the potential benefits and make a commitment to being mindful if you hope to clear your mental clutter once and for all using meditation.

Step 2: Become one with the moment

While quieting your mind of stray thoughts is certainly helpful the real goal of mindfulness meditation is to focus completely on the moment, without forming judgments about any of the things you find. When you judge an experience, it becomes far easier to dwell on it, which will take you out of the moment as a result. While avoiding judgment is easier said than done, it is a crucial step when it comes to mastering mindfulness and it definitely becomes easier with practice. When you do find yourself passing judgment don't dwell on the fact and compound the problem, but simply let the thought go and return to the moment.

Step 3: Always return to the moment

Mindfulness meditation is the art of bringing yourself back to the moment, over and over again, as many times as it takes. It is extremely easy to get lost in a given thought and pull yourself out of the moment as a result, which is why it is important to never get discouraged. Especially early on, it is perfectly normal for your mind to wander after only a few minutes of being mindful. When this happens, all you need to do is double down and, with time, you will find that the entire process becomes far easier.

Other opportunities to be mindful

Being mindful doesn't have to be limited to only when you meditate. There are many opportunities to be mindful outside of meditation. Here are some examples.

- **Showering:** While many people operate on autopilot while in the shower, you can use this opportunity to give yourself a boost of mindfulness instead. This is because the senses are already in overdrive in the shower, which means it is easier to get into the moment than it may be in other situations.

- **Exercise:** While it might seem surprising, the mental state that the body finds itself in while exercising – specifically cardiovascular exercise – is actually quite close to a state of mindfulness, which means it doesn't take much to push it over the edge. To get in the zone, consider the way your body feels as each muscle exerts itself as you push it to the limit.

- **Chores:** The repetitive nature of most chores makes them a perfect outlet for a bit of mindfulness. To make the most of these tasks, all you need to do is clear your mind beforehand and then focus on all the sensations working through the task provides you. When you are finished, consider how much better off you are now that the chore is completed and reflect on your ability to positively affect your environment.

- **Social media:** Making a more concentrated attempt to single-task will ultimately help you practice mindfulness more easily. Until you decide to do away with social media distractions completely, consider using them in a more mindful manner instead. The next time you find yourself looking through your old photographs, use that time to really remember the moment that each photograph was taken. Strain your memory and try to recall everything you can about the situation. What were the smells, the sounds, the sights? How did you feel in the moment? Really work to try and get back to that place, to the extent that you block out external stimuli.

Chapter 18:

Take Back Your Thoughts

Once you have managed to successfully what is clouding your thoughts, the next step is to work on clearing out your mental clutter by clearing your mind. Try the following to do just that.

Understand the power of distraction

Scientists out of Brown University have recently released findings from a study that shows that one of the best ways to remove unwanted thoughts from your mind is to occupy your thoughts with something else instead. The study found that the various regions of the mind could align in thought when thinking about either the right hand or the left hand but had far more difficulty thinking of both at the same time.

You can put this fact to work when it comes to taking back your thoughts from mental clutter as soon as you have identified the types of mental clutter you are dealing with. Once this is done, you will then be able to focus on what your mental clutter is trying to force you to ignore. Focusing on the underlying problem of the matter – instead of the symptoms – will make it more difficult for anything else to get through, allowing you to gate your thoughts as a result.

Utilize substitution

If you can't distract yourself from your mental clutter using cold hard facts, you may instead find success by using your imagination instead. Specifically, you may be able to convince yourself that things aren't really as bad as they seem to be by putting on your rose-colored glasses. While this might seem like a less than ideal solution, studies from Cambridge show that if you believe hard enough pretending actually activates the same region of the brain as when you know something is true. In fact, this is how lie detectors work: Lie detector tests can only detect whether someone truly believes in what they say – not whether what they say is true or not.

With this in mind, it then becomes far easier to deal with your mental clutter once you have identified it. For example, if you constantly find yourself stacking up poorly against your peers, you simply have to believe that you are good enough and your previous beliefs and comparisons will fade away. While you may not see results overnight, you may be surprised at how effective this practice can actually be as it slowly rewrites your neural pathways.

Increase physical activity

This technique is simple. If you make the time to get out and get your blood pumping, you will find it far easier to focus on the task at hand. As such, if you find yourself feeling overwhelmed by your mental clutter, you can find an easy break from the chaos by taking the time out to exercise. By physically separating yourself from the issues at hand, you will find that it is easier to mentally let go of the issue as well. As an added bonus, you will find that the extra boost of endorphins that are released at the same time will also serve to improve your mood and decrease your levels of stress.

Spend more time being grateful

When you find yourself feeling overwhelmed by all of the mental clutter that is clogging your mind, taking a few minutes to focus on all the things in your life you are grateful for can help you put everything in perspective. You may want to consider certain aspects of your life you are grateful for in the moment, or you could even simply list off the things you are thankful for. The act of simply taking stock of your needs should be enough to clear your mind, at least in the short-term, and can help you get things back on track afterwards.

Dealing with negative self-talk

When working through your mental clutter, one thing you will eventually need to deal with is any negative self-talk that you have been abetting despite your best interests. Everyone has a little voice inside that whispers that they may not be fast enough, strong enough, smart enough, etc., to complete a given task. Most people are able to keep that voice relatively quiet, but those who are dealing with lots of mental clutter have no such luck. As such, their negative self-talk runs wild, making it more difficult to clear out their mental clutter overall.

Luckily, negative self-talk can be directly countered with positive self-talk. Positive self-talk is an exercise that helps clear out the types of mental clutter that supports negative self-talk, and it can be used whenever you find yourself being particularly down on a thought or action you are attempting. To get started, all you need to do is to be aware of a negative thought that is taking place and strive to replace it with a positive thought instead. It is important that you strive to deny the thought before you replace it for the best results.

While this may not feel particularly productive at first, it is important to keep it up if you hope to see serious results. Eventually, you will find that you are able to break yourself out of negative self-talk by simply being aware of what it is your mind is trying to do. Even better, with enough practice, you will be able to replace negative self-talk with positive self-talk which will ultimately go a long way towards altering your mindset for the better.

If you find that you have a hard time with this exercise at first, don't despair; many people grew up in environments that make it difficult to express themselves without feeling awkward, you just need to persevere. If you find that you have a hard time substituting in positive thoughts for negative ones, try writing these substitutions down in a journal first to help you get the hang of it. When writing, all you need to do is look for phrases containing words like "can't" or "won't", and then you simply replace them with positive alternatives instead. With practice, this will clear your mind of all sorts of mental clutter.

Chapter 19:

Importance of Essentialism to Your Health

A chronically cluttered mind will have a major impact on your life, physically, mentally and emotionally. You may not even realize the effect it is having until you release some of this clutter. Basically, you are not seeing the forest through the trees.

Let's take a look at the physical impact first. It is often hard to relate your physical health to your mental state. Modern medicine has trained us to avoid seeing how our mental state affects our physical body, and we assume that any physical ailments we have are stand-alone problems.

In reality, our brain and body are deeply interwoven. You cannot separate one from the other. A great example of this is stress. We often think of stress as a mental thing. We feel stress from work and from keeping a tight schedule in our households. This stress not only makes us tired and unfocused, but it also wreaks havoc on our bodies. Stress raises hormones like cortisol which cause us to stress eat and gain weight. It raises our blood pressure and creates problems within the heart if left unchecked. It also affects our digestive system, creating problems like Irritable Bowel Syndrome (IBS) that are generally thought incurable by modern science.

Early physical symptoms of stress are largely ignored. Minor aches and pains can be explained away by sitting too long or sleeping on something incorrectly. In reality, stress creates an inflammatory response in the body which causes pain in joints and muscles. It is a physical manifestation of stress. It is a real thing, something that science is just beginning to pinpoint.

The inflammatory response caused by stress causes the immune system to respond. Every time we need to use our immune system to deal with this low-level inflammation, it is taking away resources used to protect the body from environmental threats like bacteria and viruses. Symptoms of stress can simply cause you to get sick more often.

As chronic stress continues, the immune system gets tired and weak. It begins to recognize similarities in harmful substances and body cells. Since it can't tell the difference, the immune system begins to attack healthy body cells, causing autoimmune diseases. This is the case in diseases like rheumatoid arthritis, multiple sclerosis and thyroid disorders like Hashimoto's. It has been scientifically proven that stress exacerbates symptoms of Lupus, another autoimmune disease. Stress is real, and it all stems from a cluttered mind.

It is difficult to grasp how mind clutter can affect the body physically, at least until science proves it. It is very easy to recognize how a cluttered mind affects us mentally, emotionally and spiritually, however.

What is the harm in that? Neglecting to live in the moment means you will be missing out on the natural interactions that happen around you. On your ride in, you missed the colors of the sunrise in your rearview mirror, or missed that cloud that looked like a bunny soaring high above you. You unwittingly cut someone off, putting another driver in a bad mood for the rest of the day. You are not present. You are not living your life.

The pressure of this life we live means that we are always waiting for the next moment to happen. We are not engaged in the now because we don't feel we have time to let it play out. Have you ever rushed a conversation with someone because you had things to do? Was it really that important that you could not focus on this person for just another thirty seconds? Did you stand there listening for that thirty seconds but didn't really hear them? What is the point?

How about technology? How often do you skip interacting with someone because you are on the phone, or scrolling through social media? Keep in mind that your inner spirit, the force that drives you, existed long before the invention of social media. It thrives on interaction with others, with movement and physical progress. It does not understand the draws of social media. You are killing your spirit by skipping out on interactions in real life in exchange for this pseudo-world we have built around ourselves. Do you really even know those "friends" you have on social media?

Living in this day and age makes us emotionally numb. Avoiding interactions at all costs means that we are not really using our emotional intelligence. Unless you are fully engrossed in how something makes you feel, you are not actually living. You are not seeing the subtle nuances of life that bring you happiness, joy and a reason to live. The small interactions and appreciation we have at any given moment are what life is all about, and we are missing it!

Take some time to really hear what someone is saying to you. Give your undivided attention and understand the world that is going on around you. Let the past be in the past, and let it go. Hold no grudges, don't let the past define you.

Chapter 20:

Tackle Your Problems Head-On

Life is challenging and often difficult and tends to throw things our way around every corner. The problem is, if this is your way of thinking, then there is a chance that you may be a little positive. Still, people face problems on a daily basis – this does not, however, mean that we should only focus on those challenges that life presents us with. Unfortunately, it can sometimes be difficult to focus on the good when there is so much negativity and bad in our lives.

When our minds are filled with negative thoughts about the challenges that are making life feel more difficult, then it causes clutter in our minds – this leads to poor performance at work, racing thoughts, and difficulty concentrating, amongst other psychological issues.

Start by Facing Reality

It can be hard to face reality sometimes which is why we often find ourselves wandering off to imagination land in order to help ourselves feel better. When we do not face reality, we are unable to face our problems – in fact, without a healthy dose of reality, how would you truly be able to see what problems are causing you to fall behind and stay behind in life.

Think long-term here. When you start facing reality for what it is, and you acknowledge the problems that are present in your life, it will be easier to face them and to solve these problems. In turn, you would be able to stop thinking about the problems constantly, significantly reducing the thoughts and memories that are cluttering your mind.

To face reality, you will need to embrace your life – just the way it is right now. Even if things are bad, know that they can be better, and then embrace what you have and how things are at the moment. Stop wishing your life would be better and daydreaming about what could be. If you do not start by embracing the present and facing up to the problems in your life, then you won't be able to move forward.

Even though facing your own reality and embracing your life, as well as identifying the problems and challenges you are facing, are all important factors in the process of truly decluttering your mind, I want to put emphasis on the fact that you should really take your time with this as well.

The last thing you want is to make things worse. Decide for sure that you are going to change, that you are going to start facing reality, but allow yourself time to adjust slowly.

It would be a good idea to have a notepad for this step. You can write down things in life that you are thinking about constantly – the challenges that you are facing, problems that are posing a threat to your happiness and, of course, your mental well-being.

Facing Your Problems, Overcoming Your Challenges

Identifying issues in your own life that are cluttering up that mind of yours is only the first step to solving them – you will need to embrace every one of these problems and then try to solve them to the best of your ability. When you have a list of such problems you need to solve and challenges that you must overcome, you will be able to determine which ones you can tackle now, and which objectives should be set aside for a later date – don't put them off and avoid delaying for too long, however.

Again, be realistic about the list you have made. Start with those issues that you can tackle right now. If you haven't spoken to a friend in a long time because the two of you had a fight a few years back, then look up their number and give them a call. Chances are, they might be feeling the same way as you do – regretting that fight and wanting to catch up with you again after all these years.

As you face these problems and overcome them one at a time, you are already starting to declutter your mind. With each problem out of the way, there are fewer issues that are constantly coming up in your mind. Negative thoughts are replaced with positive thoughts. You will start to sleep more peacefully at night. Your productivity will start to improve. And, you'll be able to start focusing on things that matter without constantly thinking of that overdue bill that might just cause you to end up with a judgment against your name.

Conclusion

As you have read, becoming an essentialist is a surefire way to becoming the happiest you have ever been in this life. As you allow more inanimate objects to define your worth, the less fulfillment you will find in the very short life we all have to live.

It's incredible to me that many people have never heard of the essentialist lifestyle, for it is how we should have been raised and taught all along. I have no doubt that your perspectives of the life you are living currently have shifted at least a degree or two as you have discovered some intriguing ways to get your life back on the right track by just allowing room for what is essential to you.

I hope that this book provided you with the necessary tools, confidence, and motivation to begin weeding your way through unnecessary things within your own life as your clear the path for success, prosperity, and freedom.

I hope that you start to put the techniques this book had to offer to use very soon, because why wait another day? Why spend another day wasted on looking after things, collecting items, and sifting your way through them attempting to find the real meaning of your life? Today is your day to begin anew!

Made in the USA
Monee, IL
02 December 2019